I0409520

WHY DO THE RICH BORROW?

BY

JUSTIN MACDONATUS

Copyright reserved. No part of this book may be copied or reproduced without the prior written permission of the author.

Contents

PREFACE

There is a common misconception that the rich don't borrow money. In fact, the opposite is often true. Many wealthy people use debt to their advantage, leveraging it to grow their businesses and acquire assets.

There are a few reasons why the rich borrow. First, they often have access to better terms than the average person. Banks and other lenders are more willing to lend money to people with high credit scores and a proven track record of success.

Second, the rich are often able to use debt to offset taxes. For example, they may borrow money to invest in real estate, which can generate depreciation deductions that reduce their taxable income.

Third, the rich understand the power of compound interest. When they borrow money, they can use it to invest in assets that appreciate over time. This can help them grow their wealth exponentially.

Of course, there is also a risk associated with borrowing money. If you're not careful, you can end up in debt that you can't repay. However, if you're smart about it, borrowing money can be a powerful tool for wealth building.

This book will explore the reasons why the rich borrow and how you can use debt to your advantage. It will cover topics such as:

How to access better terms on loans

How to use debt to offset taxes

How to invest in assets that appreciate over time

How to manage your debt so that you don't end up in financial trouble

If you're looking to build wealth, this book is for you. It will teach you how to use debt to your advantage and reach your financial goals.

I hope you find this preface helpful. I encourage you to read the rest of the book to learn more about how the rich borrow and how you can use debt to your advantage.

CHAPTER 1

WHY DO THE RICH BORROW?

Rich people borrow for a variety of reasons, including:

WE BORROW TO INVEST.

Rich people often use debt to invest in assets that they believe will appreciate in value over time. This can include real estate, businesses, or even other types of investments.

WE ALSO BORROW TO FINANCE BUSINESS EXPENSES.

Many wealthy people own businesses, and they may use debt to finance the day-to-day operations of their businesses. This can include things like inventory, equipment, or marketing expenses.

WE BORROW TO PURCHASE ASSETS THAT APPRECIATE IN VALUE.

Rich people may also borrow money to purchase assets that they believe will appreciate in value over time. This can include things like art, jewelry, or even classic cars.

WE BORROW TO CONSOLIDATE DEBT.

If a wealthy person has a lot of high-interest debt, they may use debt to consolidate that debt into a single loan with a lower interest rate. This can save them money in the long run.

WE ALSO BORROW TO GENERATE TAX BENEFITS.

In some cases, borrowing money can actually generate tax benefits for wealthy people. For example, the interest on a mortgage is tax-deductible.

IT'S IMPORTANT TO NOTE THAT NOT ALL RICH PEOPLE BORROW MONEY.

 SOME wealthy people are debt-free, and they prefer to pay for things with cash. However, for those who do borrow money, it's often a strategic decision that can help them grow their wealth.

Here are some additional reasons why rich people might borrow money:

WE BORROW TO TAKE ADVANTAGE OF LOW INTEREST RATES.

When interest rates are low, it can be a good time to borrow money. This is because the cost of borrowing will be lower, which can save money in the long run.

WE ALSO BORROW TO ACCESS LIQUIDITY.

Borrowing money can provide liquidity, which means having access to cash when you need it. This can be helpful for things like paying for unexpected expenses or making investments.

WE BORROW TO BUILD CREDIT.

Borrowing money and paying it back on time can help to build credit. This can be beneficial for things like getting a mortgage or a car loan in the future.

CHAPTER 2

THINGS THAT CAN MAKE A BORROWER REGRET?

Of course, there are also risks associated with borrowing money. If you're not careful, you could end up in debt that you can't afford to repay. That's why it's important to carefully consider your financial situation before borrowing money. If you're not sure whether or not borrowing money is right for you, it's a good idea to talk to a financial advisor.

There are a number of things that can make a borrower go sorrowing. These include:

NOT BEING ABLE TO AFFORD THE MONTHLY PAYMENTS.

This is perhaps the most common reason why borrowers go sorrowing. If you can't afford to make the monthly payments on your loan, you'll likely end up defaulting on the loan, which can have serious consequences for your credit score and your financial future.

LOSING YOUR JOB OR EXPERIENCING A FINANCIAL SETBACK.

If you lose your job or experience a financial setback, it can be difficult to make your monthly loan payments. This can lead to feelings of anxiety, stress, and sorrow.

NOT UNDERSTANDING THE TERMS OF THE LOAN.

Before you take out a loan, it's important to understand the terms of the loan, including the interest rate, the monthly payments, and the repayment period. If you don't understand the terms of the loan, you're more likely to end up in financial trouble.

FEELING OVERWHELMED BY DEBT.

If you have a lot of debt, it can be easy to feel overwhelmed and stressed. This can lead to feelings of sorrow and despair.

CHAPTER 3

WHAT TO DO IF OVERCOME BY DEBT?

If you're a borrower who is feeling sorrowing, there are a few things you can do to cope with your feelings.

FIRST, IT'S IMPORTANT TO TALK TO SOMEONE ABOUT HOW YOU'RE FEELING.

This could be a friend, family member, therapist, or financial advisor. Talking to someone can help you to feel less alone and can give you some helpful advice.

SECOND, IT'S IMPORTANT TO CREATE A BUDGET AND TO TRACK YOUR SPENDING.

This will help you to see where your money is going and to make sure that you're not overspending.

THIRD, IT'S IMPORTANT TO MAKE A PLAN TO REPAY YOUR DEBT.

This may involve consolidating your debt, negotiating with your creditors, or finding a new job.

IT'S IMPORTANT TO REMEMBER THAT YOU'RE NOT ALONE.

Millions of people struggle with debt, and there are resources available to help you. If you're feeling sorrowing, don't hesitate to reach out for help.

HERE ARE SOME ADDITIONAL TIPS FOR BORROWERS WHO ARE FEELING SORROWING

Don't give up. It may seem like a daunting task, but it is possible to overcome debt.
Just take it one step at a time and don't give up.

FOCUS ON THE POSITIVE.

It's easy to get caught up in the negative when you're struggling with debt. But it's important to focus on the positive things in your life, such as your family, your friends, and your health.

TAKE CARE OF YOURSELF.

When you're feeling stressed and overwhelmed, it's important to take care of yourself. This means eating healthy, getting enough sleep, and exercising regularly.

SEEK PROFESSIONAL HELP.

If you're struggling to cope with debt on your own, don't hesitate to seek professional help. A financial advisor or therapist can help you to develop a plan to repay your debt and to manage your stress.

CHAPTER 4

WHAT ARE ALTERNATIVES TO BORROWING?

SAVE UP FOR YOUR EXPENSES.

THIS is the most obvious alternative to borrowing, and it's often the best option. If you can save up for your expenses, you won't have to pay interest on a loan.

ASK FOR HELP FROM FRIENDS OR FAMILY.

If you're in a tight spot, you may be able to borrow money from a friend or family member. This can be a good option if you're only borrowing a small amount of money and you're confident that you can repay it.

GET A PART-TIME JOB.

If you need some extra money, you could get a part-time job. This is a good way to earn money without having to take on debt.

SELL SOME OF YOUR BELONGINGS.

If you have some unused belongings, you could sell them to raise some money. This is a good way to get rid of clutter and make some extra cash.

APPLY FOR A GRANT OR SCHOLARSHIP.

If you're struggling to pay for school or other expenses, you could apply for a grant or scholarship. These are often offered by government agencies, businesses, and charitable organizations.

USE A CREDIT CARD WITH A 0% APR INTRODUCTORY OFFER.

If you need to borrow money for a short period of time, you could use a credit card with a 0% APR introductory offer. This will allow you to borrow money without having to pay interest for a certain period of time.

It's important to weigh the pros and cons of each alternative before deciding which one is right for you. Some factors to consider include the amount of money you need, the length of time you need it, and your credit score.

CREATE A BUDGET AND STICK TO IT.

This will help you track your spending and make sure you're not overspending.

PAY OFF YOUR DEBT AS QUICKLY AS POSSIBLE.

The longer you carry debt, the more interest you'll pay.

AVOID USING CREDIT CARDS FOR EVERYDAY PURCHASES.

This will help you avoid accumulating debt.

BUILD UP YOUR SAVINGS.

This will give you a financial cushion in case of unexpected expenses.

Borrowing money can be a tempting option, but it's important to consider the alternatives before you take out a loan. There are many ways to get the money you need without having to borrow.

THANKS FOR YOU HUMILITY

IN TAKING THIS COURSE, WE KNOW
THAT YOU WERE NOT EMPTY AT
THE POINT OF ENTRY.

WE ONLY PRAY THAT THIS COURSE
REFRESH AND ADD AT THE LEAST,
ONE NEW IDEA TO YOU.

SHOULD YOU HAVE ANY FEEDBACK
ON THIS COURSE, DO NOT FORGET
TO REACH US VIA:
info@ndseminary.com

THEY SAID IT

"The invention of money opened a new field to human avarice by giving rise to usury and the practice of lending money at interest while the owner passes a life of idleness."

Pliny the Elder
- https://graciousquotes.com/lending/

NOTES

NOTES

NOTES

www.ingramcontent.com/pod-product-compliance
Lightning Source LLC
Chambersburg PA
CBHW072227290526
45794CB00007B/2918